Ramadan

Our Magical Adventure

Written By: Hend Alkarzon

Dedications:

To my parents, Manal and Awni, every success in my life is owed to you, with much love.

To my siblings, Nour, Bashar, Maha, and Mohammed, may you always find happiness wherever you go.

To my life partner, Adel, my rock and all—time supporter, you inspire me to be the best I can be.

This book is as much yours as it is mine.

With love,
Hend Alkarzon

In a colorful town, three best friends, Mohammed, Adel, and Nour, were getting ready for a special month called Ramadan. They also had a playful cat named Sugar. The moon in the sky told them it was time for a magical adventure!

Mohammed, the kind and caring friend, woke up early with his family for a special Suhoor before the sun woke up. The sky turned golden, and he felt happy that Ramadan has just started.

Adel, the playful friend, loved laughing and having fun.
He made lanterns and told funny stories with Mohammed.
Adel's happiness made their adventure more
exciting!

Nour, the curious friend, explored with Sugar. They found hidden treasures and made the adventure extra special. Nour's imagination made every moment magical for the friends.

Later, two more friends, Maha and Bashar, joined the group. They brought fun and joy, making the friends' group even better!

All friends helped others by making special gift bags with yummy snacks. They gave these gifts to people who needed them. It felt good to share and help, just like friends do in Ramadan.

When the sun went down, the friends gathered to break their fast with a yummy Iftar. They felt happy, and their friendship grew stronger with every delicious bite.

One night, the friends went to the mosque together. They wore their best clothes and stood side by side to pray Taraweeh. In the quiet and peaceful mosque, they felt close to each other and to Allah.

The friends listened to the beautiful words from the Quran during Taraweeh prayers. They stood together, feeling grateful for their friendship and the special moments they shared in Ramadan.

In the mosque, Mohammed led the group in attending Taraweeh prayers. As they listened to the beautiful recitation of the Quran, Mohammed felt a deep sense of peace.

Adel, with his playful spirit, brought joy into the group's Ramadan adventure.
His playful nature brought a delightful energy to their journey.

Nour's curiosity knew no bounds. Together with Sugar, she brought an extra touch of magic to their Ramadan adventure.

Maha and Bashar's addition to the group created a great bond. Together, they learned about the power of unity and friendship during the holy month.

As the sun dipped below the horizon, the group of friends gathered for iftar. The smell of delicious food filled the air.

As the final days of Ramadan approached, the group of friends decided to create a Ramadan lantern together. They decorated it with vibrant colors, glitter, and messages of love.

On the night of Eid al-Fitr, the group gathered in their festive clothing, excited to celebrate the end of Ramadan. They exchanged greetings of "Eid Mubarak" and shared delicious sweets with neighbors and friends.

The group of friends reflected on their Ramadan adventure, grateful for the lessons learned and the friendships strengthened.

Magical moments filled the air as the friends sat under the starry sky, sharing stories and laughter. The town sparkled with the joy of Eid.

The friends decided to release lanterns into the sky, each carrying a wish for happiness and peace. As the lanterns floated, the friends felt a deep connection to the spirit of Ramadan.

Under the twinkling stars, the group of friends whispered their thanks to the moon for the magical nights of Ramadan. The friends held hands, their hearts connected by the special bond they shared, promising to carry the spirit of Ramadan with them always.

About The Author:

Hend is a CPA, writer, and lover of all things creative. She has always been passionate about storytelling, and with "Ramadan: Our Magical Adventure", Hend invites children on an enchanting journey into the special world of Ramadan through the eyes of delightful characters. This marks Hend's second venture into the world of children's literature, following her debut, "The Bravest Hijabi."

When she's not writing, Hend enjoys spending time with her family, traveling, photographing, trying new foods, and exploring new places.
Hend hopes that this book will inspire children to embrace their differences and appreciate the beauty of diversity in all its forms.

Thank you for reading, and I hope you enjoyed this book as much as I enjoyed writing it!

Made in United States
Troutdale, OR
03/05/2025